Build
An American ARK

The strategy and method
for US Economic Revival

Ling Ling Shi

With my scared hands, with the ink mixed by blood and tears,
I share with you- Americans and US Leaders,
The Hope of Revival

iUniverse, Inc.
New York   Bloomington

Build An American ARK
The strategy and method for U.S. Economic Revival

iUniverse books may be ordered through booksellers or by contacting:

iUniverse
1663 Liberty Drive
Bloomington, IN 47403
www.iuniverse.com
1-800-Authors (1-800-288-4677)

Because of the dynamic nature of the Internet, any Web addresses or links contained in this book may have changed since publication and may no longer be valid. The views expressed in this work are solely those of the author and do not necessarily reflect the views of the publisher, and the publisher hereby disclaims any responsibility for them.

ISBN: 978-1-4401-3020-5 (pbk)
ISBN: 978-1-4401-3021-2 (ebk)

Unless otherwise indicated, Scripture is taken from the Holy Bible, New International Version®. NIV®. Copyright© 1973, 1978, 1984 by International Bible Society. Used by permission. All rights reserved.

Scripture marked NKJV is taken from the New King James Version of the Bible.

Printed in the United States of America

iUniverse rev. date: 4/3/2009

This book is dedicated to our

Heavenly Father
Lord Jesus Christ
Holy Spirit

Because you love me so deeply,
You allow darkness to approach me,
Because you love me so deeply,
You watch me walk into the darkness sorrowfully.

I want to praise, in the night, at darkness,
in the night, I see you face by face,
I want to praise, in the night, at darkness,
in the night, You pour out the blessing to me abundantly.

Because you love me so deeply,
You allow darkness to approach me,
Because you love me so deeply,
You watch me walk into the darkness sorrowfully.

I want to praise, in the night, at darkness,
in the night, I see your glorious presences,
I want to praise, in the night, at darkness,
in the night, You walk with me !

This book is a loving gift to

My Father

Father, thank you, even you don't like to express, but I know you love me, you worry about me in the past decades. I can see your strength within, I learn from it, you were very sick, but you don't want me and mother to worry, you always answer us: "I am alright". When I was facing great suffering, you understood, because you are my father even I don't tell. Your hand tapping my hand with loving silence, I can feel you cry for me in your heart. I saw your hand drawing a cross in your heart with silence, that is your deep faith, you pray for me with silence, but my heart can feel your love and care for me. May this book can bring joy and comfort to you, my father.
Thanks for the days you are with me.

My Mother

Mother, thank you, for the past over four decades, you love me with all your heart , especially in the past two years, in my life storm and the trial, you stand with me by your love, encouragement, support and pray. Without you, I hardly can image how I can overcome so many difficulties, so much sorrow, you are a angel of God , stand with me , help me, strengthen me.
Mother, this weak and small family, today, can stand here strong and brave, one of the main reasons is your consistently pray and steadfast faith in Lord Jesus Christ.
Mother, the days we cried together, we laughed together, we dreamed together, we prayed together, we hugged each other , we shared the love of God ,will always be in my memories as the beauties which God grant to me.
I love you with my deep thanks.

Contents

Dear Americans and U.S. Leaders:

Today, as a single mother with two young children, a daughter of ageing parents, a foreign student from China 20 years ago, a person with different multiple experiences being an employee and employer in various industries, a person who had made a series of serious mistakes, a sinner saved by Gospel of Jesus Christ, a U.S. citizen, I present the book "Build an American ARK" with my gratitude in our country's economic crisis.

Despite the worrisome news surrounding our nation, through pray and think, I can see a tremendous powerful economic force and chance behind all the negative scenes for our nation. May this book help our country in someway.

I never thought that someday I would write a book regarding economic topics or issues. Life journey is amazing, the Love of God always leads me to the realm which I never dreamed of.

Since I shut down my newspaper publishing business in the year 2000, I have rarely read any news. The lessons and failures on my business, the hurting experiences and healing processing always kept me in a lonely island.

But, in October of 2008, unceasing breaking news on financial institution crisis, especially in several major investment banks as well as the government's $700 billion dollars bailout plan caught my attention, an economic war beginning from U.S.A. and spreading to other nations shook the world.

Behind the scenes of the war, I saw the poison roots of economic crisis in U.S.A. which is so similar to what happened within my private businesses. I realized what U.S. government and American families suffered are the same as mine.

I started to pray that our country can able to content and solve the nation's economic crisis. The more I pray, the more courage I got from the deep of my heart to walk out from my personal island and participate the challenge and the battles to conquer the economic crisis.

The management principle on nation is as same as that on families and enterprises, because they share many aspects.

Driven by the worry for our nation, by the desire in my heart to help the other hurting souls, I started to accept the desire from the deep of my heart to write this book.

In the past two decades, I have been facing my personal red sea again and again, I have been wandered and circled in the wilderness and desert day by day. Since my personal life's confusion, my family was falling apart and my businesses ended with general debts and tax debts, my life seemed totally miserable and hopeless. Thanks to God, His grace saves me, His mercy forgives me, His strength lifts me up, His truth lights on me and guides me, His unconditional love makes me turn my miserable and hopeless life into full of hope and faith.

The past several months were so memorable and precious to me, this unexpected writing journey healed my remaining sorrows, melted my remaining pains, taught me the further message of forgiveness, directed me to walk into the deep of the Truth of God, practice more deep in the Word of God. This precious journey led me experience the fire of Hope being poured out from heaven to earth abundantly upon me and this book.

Now, with a free soul and peace in Truth of God , I present the citizen's book " Build an American ARK" based on my previous experiences, thinking, study, researching , observation and pray.

I believe learning is a life time process; I believe that mistakes and failures could become our stepping stones to higher levels; I believe that our country is full of the hope because of God, no matter how many difficulties we are facing now; I truly believe that He never leaves

His children alone. May His blessing of wisdoms pour upon Americans and U.S. Leaders and lead us out of confusion and crisis.

In the midst of economic crisis storms, to U.S. leaders, the burdens and responsibilities are tremendous. May Lord protect the leadership team and guide them by His wisdoms and strength them to lead the United States of America from crisis to victory. May the Americans and U.S. government be more than conquerors!

Faithful and Truly

Ling Ling Shi
California, U.S.A.

"**Ask and it will be given to you; seek and you will find; knock and the door will be opened to you. For everyone who asks receives; he who seeks finds; and to him who knocks, the door will be opened.**"

(Matthew: 7:7)

Theme I

Discover the Treasure of U.S.A.

"The Lord is my rock, my fortress and my deliverer;
my God is my rock, in whom I take refuge.
He is my shield and the horn of my salvation,
my stronghold."

(Psalm 18:2)

INTRODUCTION

Touched by a banner

One day in October, 2008, when I sat in a waiting hall of county's medical office, there was a small banner which caught my eyes on the wall:

No Shame
No Blame
No Name

I was touched deeply by this small banner, a gratitude to this nation's will to encourage, care and love people came out from my heart. My soul can see that the spirit behind the small banner is Love of God, the spirit behind is the same as the most of pilgrim's spirit who seek and followed the Faith on Lord and Savior Jesus Christ and lived a meaningful life for God and for people.

Turning my mind to many realities on this nation which are opposite to the message on this banner, I think over and over, what happened to this country that in the deep has such beauties? Why are there so much difficulties and obstacles for U.S. government to fulfill the dream and responsibilities to all Americans? Why are there so many families suffer as well as U.S. government suffers in this fertile and vast land? Why the American dream is so distant to millions of us?

I had lived in a blurry and confused American dream for many years, I built my dream foundation on the sand and worked hard on it. After years and years laboring, sufferings and emptiness followed my life. In the period of desperation, I found the most precious Love of God, Jesus Christ. Since that on, the lose is no longer lose, the regret is no longer regret, the pain is no longer pain----- all of them when be linked together, became a tunnel where I walked through from the dark to the Light, from confusion to Truth of God, from being hopeless to full of Hope.

The more I appreciated the chance this country gave to me to meet the Light of God in this amazing land, the more I care this country's soul; The more I feel there are many beloved hidden treasure which was directly stored by our Loving God in this country, the more I want to become a farmer to care and work on the field.

I felt worry and sorrow for U.S.A since I started to observe different areas in this country, especially, when this great economic crisis took place in this country and spread to the whole world. The more I examine the root of crisis, the more urgency I feel.

I look at the sufferings of U.S. government who is ordained by God to take care of Americans, I can see the nation's crisis that in my old shadow, in which I was the miniature once deeply in suffer and sorrow on a micro scope of financing turmoil. I can not deny my inner voice which urge me to help this giant – U.S. government in someway and somehow. I went through the valley of the shadow of death, I can't deny my inner voice and fake my heart to ignore the fact, the giant-U.S. government who originally has such beautiful heart and dream which reflected in that small banner, is walking in the similar valley.

The banner is small, but the signal is so significant to me, I have to speak the truth to help this nation which was built upon the dream of Faith in Lord Jesus Christ, no more confusions and fears!

> **"Even though I walk through the valley of**
> **the shadow of death, I will fear no evil,**
> **for you are with me;**
> **Your rod and your staff, they comfort me"**
>
> **(Psalm 23:4)**

This was King David's testimony in Psalm, it was written from the hero's heart, the hero was in great danger, but he never stop to love the Almighty God, he never intentionally hurt God through bad deeds, he lived in the sweet love with God, he kept God in his heart and lip, he confessed and apologized to God when he realized that his mistakes and sinful deeds were against God, he was like a beloved child on the arms of God, he sung, he danced, he praised, he thanked, he sought, he followed in the presence of God unceasingly, that's why he could "walk in the valley of shadow of death and fear no evil".

Can we experience the same as King David?

Yes, we can, God is same, yesterday, today and forever! If we lift our eyes to the sky like King David to seek the Truth of God, if we aim our eyes on God alone and have a relationship between a father and a son, we will experience the same as King David.

For the love to this country and people, for the love to hundreds of millions my brothers and sisters in Lord Jesus Christ , for the thanks to God who brought me out of dark tunnel, I am going to speak the truth. I hope our nation can truly experience the same journey like King David and sing the Psalm 23 as if written by Americans and U.S.A. leaders.

**"You prepare a table before me in the
presence of my enemies.
You anoint my head with oil; my cup overflows.
Surely goodness and love will follow me
all the days of my life,
and I will dwell in the house of the Lord forever"**

(Psalm 23: 5~6)

This is my favorite Psalm and Bible verses. In the valley of the shadow of death, I often sung the Psalm 23 like singing my own poem and song. May my testimony carry you to a realm full of hope to discover the true strength and wisdom in personal life and in our nation to overcome the economic crises.

———— Ling Ling's testimony and hope ————

I have countless testimonies for the Gospel of Lord and Savoir Jesus Christ. In this book, today, I want to share with you one of my testimonies which is directly related to economic sector.

Seeking American dream

Year 1988, I left my engineering teacher's career in an aviation college, from China to U.S.A. for the opportunity to pursue higher education and seek the American dream. After I finished my MBA, I continually pursued the so-called America dream, a blurry and confusing concept in my heart.

I formed an import business in 1994, the business was established on an unhealthy basis from the beginning, and there was no concept on my mind that a business must be operated under a discipline and lawful financial management system no matter what size it is in.

Lack of experiences in business to projecting and budgeting, business operation's overall cost can not be covered by revenue, our initial contribution was gone quickly, the financial condition started turn from bad to worse. In order to cover the deficits and continue business, I had to borrow money from different sources such as credit card and loans. Due to soaring deficits, the company's finance situation and system gradually fell to big mess.

The money from loans was never enough to cover the shortage, the financial black hole got bigger and bigger and there were no way to patch it anyhow. No matter how hard I worked for, it just didn't work. The longer I stayed in business, the bigger pressure and measure of debts. After several years struggle, the corporation financial condition was totally broken in debts, my health condition was broken too, I got seriously depression in year 1997.

I didn't want to file bankruptcy due to my face and wish that I will make the business work to pay the all debts and responsibilities. Technically, the business was bankrupt, I just didn't want to accept the reality.

I kept telling myself there are hopes on business, don't give up; I encouraged myself to have confidence to win the dream; I forced myself to work hard even I was very sick; I carried the heavy burdens from personal to business on my shoulders and continuously barely ran with some unknown and unexplainable hope deeply hidden in my heart.

Born Again in Jesus Christ

Just in that dark tunnel, facing all kinds brokenness from business to personal life and heart emptiness, I was touched by a beautiful dream and heard a sweet melody from heaven above, I followed the new dream and melody, I found and accepted Jesus Christ as my Lord and Savior in Nov. 28, 1999.

Keep falling

In order to keep my dream of perfection and take care my responsibilities, I kept running the race in business sector even though I failed; I could not accept the facts as a failure; I failed, I stood up again, I failed, I stood up once more----- year after year, I tried my best and worked hard to find any breakthrough in business to patch previous financial black hole.

I put my efforts to develop business, but one key area that I ignored the importance was to set up restrict rule for company's operation system, especially accounting system. This seriously weakness in business was never changed or taken care of. The unhealthy system caused the black hole bigger and bigger.

The race kept on, the business kept lose.

Since I became a follower of Jesus Christ, I started living in a mixed and more conflicting life from that point. Many unexplainable reasons and excuses heavily bond my mind and my tiny new life, I did not escape from financial chaos which was built up by several years unhealthy business behavior and environment, accumulated heavy burden by years deficits, to make things worse, in year 2001, I walked into a bigger financial turmoil and chaos.

Failed in temptations

A deep trap was under my feet, I kept falling to a poison trap.

Beginning of year 2001, I formed a new retail furniture business based on credit lines from several vendors. The new business kept the same behavior of mess in financial management. In comparison with other small businesses, the difference was that the furniture retail business not only was built in same pattern, but also, faced some temptations I never faced before.

One of the big temptations was retail sales tax. As time passed by, it was really bother me when I realize that the Truth of God prohibits such un-Godly business behaviors. I fought, I struggled, I compromised and I failed on this very important issue.

Accepting the bargain from consumers not to pay sales tax became one of our retail business's usual way to catch the sales; hiding the retail sales volume to avoid paying extra sales tax became a way to save some money to make business afloat and survival.

Looking back on it, I deeply know that I had denied Lord hundreds times during that six years furniture retail business operation if Apostle Peter had denied Lord three times.

If I realized the mess up and undisciplined financial system was wrong and killed business's dignity before I saw the Light of God, yet, after I was saved by Gospel, the fact that I still lived in fears, compromised and accepted sinful conducts in business were my undeniable and inexcusable mistakes and faults as a born-again-child of Jesus Christ.

Inside strong fights and battles

My heart was pounding when I committed sins and allow business financial system operated in mess.

Unspeakable battles and fights between the Word of God and my secular life took place. These kinds of severe battles and fights never happened before when I was a non-believer and idol worshiper, I knew that I became quite different than before, my soul rebuke my flesh all the time, the Word of God remained alive incredibly.

"We know that the law is spiritual; but I am unspiritual, sold as a slave to sin"

(Roman: 7:14)

The more sins I committed, the more guiltiness and fears I got. I know somehow I need to work hard with Jesus Christ to set me free indeed, because from first day I met with Him, I believe that He has the life changing power.

I was kidnapped by sins and kept living in bondage. I really want to be free, I long and pray for a new life indeed. I tried, I tried to work with Jesus, to follow the Word of God in dealing with several un-Godly issues in my business sector, but, at the very last step, I withdrew by the unspeakable fears.

For the purpose to patch the financial black hole, I kept choosing to listen to the flesh rather than take the Word of God and cut the shackles of sins in my neck and feet. I can't explain why I was so blind and deaf in years when I deal with my business issues. I woke up after I did something wrong, I fell to sleep again, my mind was played by evil spirit consistently. I walked back and forth between light and dark, right and wrong, I was tempted and failed again and again.

"So I find this law at work: When I want to do good, evil is right there with me. For in my inner being I delight in God's law; but I

9

see another law at work in the members of my body, waging war against the law of my mind and making me a prisoner of the law of sin at work within my members. What a wretched man I am! "

(Roman: 7:21~24)

My realities often mocked my faith, my unclean life often made fun on me. I feel deadly sorry and sorrow to my Lord Jesus Christ who died for my sins at cross. It made me feel so guilty to God that I compromised with wrong business behaviors to sustain business by sacrifice my faith and belief.

Two of me fight all the time!

There are many ways to escape from punishment or penalty from earthly laws, but there is no any way to escape from Word of God. Wherever I run, the Word of God follows my heart and speak to me-a sinner longs for changing.

During that period of big confliction, the Word of God was alive and kept working on me. Walking in the gloomy circumstances of mess business which could kill my faith, Lord gave me dreams with encouragements and wisdoms to lift my Faith and Hope, also, He amazingly gave me songs to sing out my sorrows, pains, deeply thanks and grateful praise in my lonely island. Someway and somehow He always lets me know He is with me and loves me. I failed Him, but He never leaves me alone and never withdraws His presence. That is why, in the midst of storms in my life, although failed in temptations and paralyzed in trials, I still have strong Faith and Hope in Him. The strong Faith and Hope has never changed no matter what mess I was in; The strong Faith and Hope kept me to run and run although my realities show there is no hope.

The still small voices and loving whispers consistently reached me to wake me up, but every last minus and last step, I always got fears to take a breakthrough. Different kinds of fears hinder my feet to walk into a new way to conduct business, different noises told me: where I stayed is not the pit of sins, it is a chance from God to patch financial black hole, it is a blessing place from God no matter it does not look like or feel like so. The noises confused me and deceived me. As a young follower of Jesus Christ, God was still invisible in my reality world, but my black hole was visible, touchable and fearful to me.

Once upon a time, I used to be a perfectionist, but, after years in business, my life became totally upside down and with big joke and big mess. When I look at myself, I saw my body was covered by all kinds of ugly graffiti. When I walk in the valley of the shadow of death, I often experience that moment in which one of my hand received comfort, peace, encouragement and blessings, in the meantime, my another hand was placed pressures , threats, discouragements and curses by force. Often, I experienced that same moment as Elijah sat under a broom tree praying for death:

"I have had enough, Lord, take my life"----

(1 King 19:4)

The more I want to clean that ugly graffiti on me, the more mess up I got. All the efforts from my flesh strength just didn't work at all. Time passed by so quickly, the ugly and dark black hole still remained there and mocked my Faith.

The more I know my Savior, His Love, His Holiness, His righteousness, His justice, His forgiveness, His patience, His mercy, His grace, His highest law, His purpose on cross, the more tears, sorry, pain, sorrow, guiltiness, confession and regret came to my heart and soul. The battles and fights inside me between right and wrong, righteousness and evil, life and death became stronger and stronger. I cry out to my Savior for breakthrough, I cry out to my Savior for strength to receive breakthrough. I want to be free and free indeed in Jesus Christ!

**"Who will rescue me from this body of death?
Thanks be to God-through Jesus Christ our Lord!"**

(Roman 7:24~25)

I surrender all

The still small voice and encouragement whispers reached me frequently from the beginning of July 2007 and gave me strength to take operation on cancer which was in my mind to remove my fears and bondages for breakthrough.

**"He reached down from on high and took hold of me;
he drew me out of deep waters"**

(Psalm: 18:16)

I made decision to close my retail furniture business in July 14, 2007 after years battles, I could not stand myself to displease my beloved Lord Jesus Christ anymore , He was so patiently in the past seven years for my return to Truth of God, how can I deny Him again and again and remaining myself in blind and deaf? No, I can't stand sitting in pit anymore. I surrender myself to follow the will of Lord Jesus Christ no matter the future in my flesh eyes was so fearful.

That day, I told my mother about company's un-Godly business operation behaviors, I told my mother my decision to close that retail business which is my weak family's financial source. My mother supported me to follow Lord Jesus Christ no matter what the cost might be, she said this is a decision I should have made long time before, but it is never too late if I trust Him and follow Him, He will give me a another chance! Thanks to God, let my mother stood with me like a visible angel.

That day, I wrote a letter to everyone in company regarding my thinks and decision, I felt the shackle of fears left me, my soul started to feel free and shining.

Early in the morning on Sunday, July 15, 2007, awake in bed, my mother was suddenly taken into a vision: in a dark tunnel toward the light, my mother not only saw me, but also saw Lord Jesus Christ and heard His voice: "I give her a way toward the light, tell her to be calm and still in considering and conducting any work, to think about the big picture."

My mother told me the vision and the Word from the Lord. I understood the first sentence, the Lord affirmed my resolution to thoroughly leave the un-Godly business; yet when I faced extremely difficult situations, I failed to pay attention to and apply the second and third sentences. Later when I handled the whole procedure to close the business, I experienced unprecedented difficulties and temptations.

Looking back on it, I deeply feel that the spiritual war of a follower of Jesus is beyond my imagination and preparation, it is not an alarming talk that the path is full of traps, it is a comprehensive war between the truly real world and the invisible world. However, I experienced it myself, no matter how young my spiritual life is, that I may "failed to be calm and still, failed to think about the big picture," in another word, I did not understand the Word the Lord gave to me, nevertheless He listened to my prayers along the way, accompanied me through that difficult and stormy road. I was able to deeply experience the promises God gives us in the Bible.

It is true that God does not promise that we will not face any storm, but he promises that in the stormy road, he will walk with those children who rely on him, to get through the storms, and to make them more mature and strong.

Ling Ling's hope

"My grace is sufficient for you"

(2 Cor: 12:9)

It is true that His grace is sufficient for us to run the race. Along the way, the Lord never left me alone. He continuously trains my patience and endurance, He continuously cleans up my spiritual confusion, and gradually, He reveled to me the treasures in my life as gifts from God which has been saved for me by the Lord.

In my time of setbacks, I started to put the colorful puzzle pieces, which are in the wrapped gift boxes, together. I discovered the picture little by little, piece by piece, and I realized:

"Yes, Father, for this was your good pleasure."

(Matthew: 11:26)

The Word of God, the Love from God pushed me out of the pit and lifted me to a new realm with unexpected dreams.

"There I will give her back her vineyards,
and will make the Valley of Achor a door of hope"

(Hosea: 2:15)

Yes, in the vineyards He gave to me, I lean on my hope, work on my field and sing my new songs one after another.

My testimony told you of a sinner's story who died in sins and saved by Lord Jesus Christ. You may have similar experiences as me and are afraid to walk out from fear or guilt. My brothers and sisters in the Lord, my friend, don't be afraid. The Lord always gives us a second chance back to a meaningful life which God planned in our heart from the beginning. For our loving Lord, stand out, walk out from the darkness; Let our lives be a true testimony of the Gospel, and to help the souls who are in emptiness and brokenness; Let's share the Hope of Gospel with their lonely and fearful hearts.

The financial black holes we are facing may be big, but, our Hope is just standing behind the scenes of crisis. the Word of God will give us wisdom, strength and new life to move the mountain of crisis, to stop the storm of destroy.

God is Love, God is forgiveness, God is mercy, God is a sinner's second chance and only hope, God is our destiny!

**"Therefore do not let sin reign in your mortal body
so that you obey its evil desires. Do not offer the
parts of your body to sin, as instruments of
wickedness, but rather offer yourselves to God,
as those who have been brought from death to
life; and offer the parts of your body to him as
instruments of righteousness. For sin shall not be
your master, because you are not under law, but under Grace"**

(Roman: 6:12~14)

I've found new life and a real hope in Jesus Christ, I have no fears to face the previous financial black hole or turmoil; I have confidence to take care all my responsibilities; I have Faith, follow Him, to fulfill the life which God has designed for me.

My dream and desire is to become a real follower of Jesus Christ rather than a defeated soul; my dream and desire is to become an honored citizen in the sight of God rather than live in a dishonest and undisciplined life; my dream and desire is to please Him with my new songs.

How great it is to have the freedom in the Truth of God, to have a real Liberty in the Word of God, to pursue a real American dream which the Lord Jesus Christ has planned for me, to have Him as my personal Lord and Savior and dearest friend, to run the life races with Him side by side!

The Truth of God set me free, and free indeed!

During the life journey, the trials will never stop on the path to our heavenly home. Though the temptations from Satan will never stop, but:

"For God so loved the world that He gave His one and only Son, that whoever believes in Him shall not perish but have eternal life."

(John: 3:16)

If an ordinary girl and a very weak family can have such privilege to have God's love, care and guidance, how great about him! He is the God who is worthy for me to sell everything to buy the most precious holy oil for Him!

"Those whom I love I rebuke and discipline. So be earnest, and repent "

(Revelation 3: 19)

We have the same Hope

Through my personal life's path of change, I believe the Gospel of Jesus Christ has the absolute power to wake up and bring back the sinful souls to the Light. I believe that if we keep in Faith, the Truth of God will guide and shine upon the U.S. 300 million souls with His Love and Care, and lead us to the real prosperities.

Once I was a non-believer and idol worshipper, was blind and deaf, and was lost and confused, I know how wonderful the Gospel of Jesus Christ is after I tasted the living water and experienced the life changing powers. There is no doubt for me that nothing and nobody can compare with Jesus Christ, the only begotten Son of God.

God's Love reaches everywhere and everyone

My mother was a middle school teacher in China. In year 2003, on Christmas Day, she received the Holy Bible from me. She sat on the patio, and read the event of Jesus Christ's crucifixion and resurrection. Mother was deeply touched by the Holy Spirit and had accepted Jesus Christ in her heart as her personal Lord and Savior. Thanks to God, my father was saved too.

My mother told me later that if every child can have the Holy Bible to read, it'd be easy to raise and lead children in the right direction. It's wonderful to have the Word of God to teach our young generations to respect and appreciate life and to fulfill a meaningful life. As an educator, my mother thinks every child should be taught the Word of God, to have the highest moral standards and goals.

I feel the same way. When I was first touched by the Holy Spirit, I was so grateful for an ordinary life where I can see and have a relationship with God. I often talk to the Lord, about why He let me wander and circle for so long time without knowing him. If I could have come to him earlier, I would surely not have committed so many sinful deeds. But, God has His own agenda, and whatever He does, whatever He allowed, it is for the good of us!

"He restores my soul,
He guides me in paths of righteousness,
for his name's sake"

(Psalm 23:3)

Yes, I feel the same way as King David. When I put God first, when I focus on him alone, I can feel His guidance and his teachings have

17

never left me. He is just like a father who watches and cares for his child every step. Truly, who can understand me more than him? No one.

The most precious gift to children is the news of Gospel

Raising my two children, I often feel pressured, because the world is so complicated now and moral standards keep dropping. I look back at the years without knowing the Word of God or without sacrificing my life to the Truth, I had run a foolish circle and made so many mistakes. I know the temptations of the world are powerful, complex and dangerous. As a single mother, I am too weak to keep my children safe by myself.

How can I protect my children? How can I know my children are safe? The answer for me is I have support from above, and that support is Lord Jesus Christ; He is my children's best educator, because he created them. In addition to trying to become a role model for my children, I pray to my Lord Jesus Christ, who loves them more than I do, to lead them in this complex world to learn what ever they need to learn, to experience what ever they need to experience. I believe that burdens and trials are our wings, on them we will soar to the realm of blessing.

Americans have the best in the universe

On my Faith journey, I deeply realized that there are several things in the world that nothing else can compare and be equal to:

First, no idols can compare and be equal to the Heavenly Father, He is above all.
Second, no religion can compare and be equal to the Lord Jesus Christ, He is above all.
Third, no other spirit can compare and be equal to the Holy Spirit, He is above all.

This realization make me full of appreciations to God, He give himself to this very tiny life.

Our Heavenly Father, Lord Jesus Christ and the Holy Spirit are above all! It is our nation's wonderful privilege to have Him as our nation's Faith, to building nation's foundation upon the Rock of Ages, to have God directly intervene, teach and guide his children who follow him sincerely and humbly.

How great and blessed we are! We really need to appreciate the blessings and do not down-grade our faith to line up with low worldly standards of those who have never tasted the living water of Jesus Christ.

Dear brothers and sisters in the Lord, compared with many other nations, we are living in an incredibly free environment. We need to appreciate what God gave to us. Give God our thanks and praise!

> **"You, dear children, are from God and have overcome them, because the one who is in you is greater than the one who is in the world."**
>
> **(1 John 4:4)**

— Inspiration from U.S. President Inauguration —

January 20, 2009, I sat in front of TV to watch the 44th US President Inauguration. I was touched by that moment when the President placed his hand in Holy Bible and lifted his right hand to take oath. It made me think.

The Precious Inheritance in USA

When the hand was placed on the Holy Bible, I saw the 44 hands of US Presidents touch the thousands of letters from our Heavenly Father, Lord Jesus and Holy Spirit, I saw the 44 hands of US Presidents touch the thousands of promises from the Old and New Testaments. For thousands of years, this Holy Bible has led God's children from generation to generation in the world; This Holy Bible has led pilgrims, 44 US Presidents and Americans for almost four hundred years in this beautiful land.

The moment of refreshment and empowerment that we all need

When the President's hand touched the Holy Bible, the Old Covenant and New Covenant between human beings and God, I felt the promises, encouragements and teachings from God flow from the Holy Bible into the President's hand, into every Americans' heart, and into whole world. This is not just any ordinary ceremony, this Inauguration is a replenishment of strength from God; This Inauguration is a chance and moment where God reminds all of us to remember the relationship and love between human beings and Him.

Seeing the President's hand touch the Holy Bible and taking the oath in front of the world, I felt that any ordinary being can have the privilege of receiving the blessing from our Heavenly Father, Lord Jesus Christ and the Holy Spirit. The Old Testament tells us the Love of God, and the New Testament tells us of His unconditional and everlasting Love and the Salvation of God that had been fulfilled through Jesus Christ.

Let's celebrate and be blessed everyday and everywhere

Seeing the President have the privilege and honor to touch the Holy Bible and take the oath in front of the whole world, I saw every American having the same privilege and honor. I was dreaming at that moment, within U.S.A., every day and everywhere, there can be such an Inauguration between God' children and God as spiritual refreshments; I was dreaming at that moment, in the homes, in churches, in schools, at work, in the courts, in the government' offices, in shopping centers, in transportation facilities, in the army, in the prisons--- in everywhere, Americans holding the Holy Bible and praying freely to our Heavenly Father, Lord Jesus Christ and Holy Spirit, if they wanted to.

I believe, with the U.S. President Inauguration, from the President to ordinary people, we all received strength, encouragement, teachings and hope from God. How great it would be to have this ceremony every day and everywhere!

While the U.S.A. faces tremendous economic crisis, let's all hold the Holy Bible like our President at the Inauguration, pray and receive strength from God, without shame, without hesitation, without fear, without doubts, without bondage, to lift hands and hearts to receive Word of God, strength, blessing, love and all he has stored for us. Let us withdraw God's grace daily with gratitude and praise.

**"I will say of the Lord, He is my refuge and
my fortress, my God, in whom I trust"**

(Psalm: 91:2)

──── U.S.A. is an amazing country ────

U.S.A. is an amazing country. The greatest and most amazing thing about the U.S.A. is her Foundation; the Faith, Love and Hope in Jesus Christ. This foundation is the Rock of Ages; This foundation is our nation's real treasure, strength and attraction. This foundation has been built up in this land by Lord himself through pilgrims.

What make U.S.A. so unique in the world?

The U.S.A. is a very special and unique nation. The first difference and distinguished character is our Foundation in Faith. Why?

Observe the other nations around the world, and you'll see that most other nations do not have an obvious spiritually established foundation. They live and operate from generation to generation based on tradition, culture or religions which had been created through thousands of years of wandering, guessing, and wishing etc. In those nations, the people seek the Truth unceasingly for thousands of years. Some countries were built upon a background in a faith that was built up through hundreds to thousands of years rather than the U.S.A., which was established in Jesus Christ from the beginning.

What makes the U.S.A. so strong?

Why can't the other nations, which have thousands of years of history, compare with the four hundred years of the U.S.A.? Why can this young nation surpass all other nations? Have you ever thought about that and found an answer?

I did. I kept thinking about the question and answers, and the answer is because the U.S.A. has the strongest foundation: the Rock of Ages, Jesus Christ!

U.S.A. has a more powerful Nation's Foundation than any other nations, U.S.A. has a more powerful Nation's Foundation than Liberty; U.S.A. has a more powerful assurance to apply Liberty in the right direction to benefit every one's life, the Powerful Power in this young nation is Gospel of Jesus Christ. But, in the past several decades, more and more souls were getting lose of memories about our nation's foundation in Lord Jesus Christ, deceived by false religions which are prohibited by our Heavenly Father, got more and more fear from to boldly claim who we are by the oppress from false liberals and different kinds of dark forces, gradually move nation's body from Rock of Ages to sand! Oh, what's the confusions and fears, they are take our nation's strength and blessing away! It's great dangerous and great lose for our nation! We need wake up! We need our souls revival first to bring our economic revival!

> **"Fear not, for I have redeemed you;**
> **I have summoned you by name;**
> **you are mine.**
> **When you pass through the water,**
> **I will be with you;**
> **and when you pass through the rivers,**
> **they will not sweep over you.**
> **When you walk through the fire,**
> **you will not be burned;**
> **the flames will not set you ablaze."**

> **(Isaiah:43:1~2)**

This is the loving promise from our Lord and Savior. Believe in Him, trust Him and be with Him. Only He has the power that can bring us out from spiritual and physical crisis!

Appreciation to God will keep our nation blessed

I believe that if Americans can sincerely recognize all the grace and favors from God, we would appreciate and protect what we have and never lose it from our hands.

I long to see Americans sing this song from generation to generation, to remember the goodness and holiness of our Lord:

> **"As for God, his way is perfect; the word of**
> **the Lord is flawless. He is a shield for**
> **all who take refuge in Him.**
> **For who is God besides the Lord?**
> **and who is the Rock except our God?**
> **It is God who arms me with strength**
> **and makes my way perfect.**
> **He makes my feet like the feet of a deer;**
> **he enables me to stand on the heights.**
> **He trains my hands for battle;**
> **my arms can bend a bow of bronze.**
> **You give me your shield of victory,**
> **and your right hand sustains me;**
> **You stoop down to make me great."**

(Psalm: 18:30~35)

This Psalm has belonged to us once upon a time. This Psalm was written as if it were for Americans. Let's sing the Psalm together unceasingly to express our appreciations to our Heavenly Father, Lord Jesus and Holy Spirit and stand on the Rock of Ages.

Build up a harmonious relationship between states and churches

**"For to us a child is born, to us a son is given,
and the government will be on his shoulders.
And he will be called
Wonderful Counselor, Mighty God,
Everlasting Father, Prince of Peace."**

(Isaiah: 9:6)

A harmonious relationship is our nation's strength

God's promise never changed, it's already done. By the Grace of Lord Jesus Christ, we came to this continent and established the U.S.A., the nation with a beautiful dream and heart. No matter how many obstacles we were faced, the strength came from Faith within this nation was never taken away before.

Upon the Rock of Ages, in the past hundreds of years, the U.S. government has gotten stronger and stronger, the abilities of this nation have gotten stronger and stronger, and the churches of Jesus Christ and its communities have gotten stronger and stronger. Once upon a time, there was a harmonious relationship between states and churches of Jesus Christ, it made this very young nation reached amazing levels of development in every area, like a child that grows into a strong man, from nobody to a world champion. When I think about all of this, I can see how much our Lord loves us, patiently and unconditionally.

God remembers who we are

We may have failed his name, we may have denied his name after the pilgrims crossed the Atlantic ocean and landed on this promised land, the same as Israel in the wilderness and desert after they crossed the red sea by the power of God, keep complaining to Moses and God, keep worshiping the idols, keep denying and hurting our Heavenly Father's heart, but, God never left Israel alone, His everlasting love kept them march on, in the past almost four hundred years, Lord Jesus Christ never withdraw His hands with nail scared, He answers His children's prays, He counsels His children's daily life, He never leave us alone no matter you feel it's like or not.

God hears and answers our prayers

God's children and churches pray for this nation unceasingly. With these prayers, the country has kept moving forward and growing.

Without the churches of Jesus Christ, without messages of salvation preached, as a sinner, I would certainly still live in blindness and deafness; I would still live in darkness and hopeless; I would not know of repentance and a second chance. I have many thanks for God for having so many churches and millions of God's children pray for the people, the government and its leaders. This is another great and amazing fact that makes this country amazing. The unceasing prayers have brought the blessing from heaven down to this land and the people that live here. How great it is!

The whole body can not be separated

I always thought that the U.S. government and the churches of Jesus Christ and its communities should have a wonderful harmonious relationship, because in God's eyes we are parts of His Body, we have different issues and areas to handle. One is the physical part, and the other is the spiritual part; We have different abilities, one is the management of nation, one is the counselor of souls; We have different responsibilities, one is to take care of peoples' secular life, one is to take care peoples' spiritual life. All is for God and God's children.

"And we know that in all things God works for the good of those who love him"

(Romans: 8:28)

In a human being's life, either spiritual life or physical life, we need both and none can be omitted. We need both to be healthy. Only both of them healthy can make us whole. Otherwise, we may be paralyzed for life.

"Come to me, all you who are weary and burdened, and I will give you rest"

(Matthew: 11:28)

As a sinner who was rescued and changed in life in Jesus Christ, I believe if the U.S. government and the communities of Faith can have a harmonious relationship without a man made wall, God will work on the both sides for good. God is Almighty, trust Him and depend on Him. He will let the U.S. government became the churches' ally and the churches of Jesus Christ will become the government's greatest help in executing the tasks which have been ordained by the Almighty God for His earthly children.

There is no one or entities perfect, we all have weaknesses. Government has its weaknesses, churches have their weaknesses, because we all face temptations and trials, while we run the races.

During the races, if we cheer each other, we help each other, we comfort each other, we lift each other, we encourage each other, we admire each other, we appreciate each other, we discover the beauties in others, we strength each other, we bless each other, and we pray for each other, then we will win the races.

Pleasing God with unity in Jesus Christ

I have always imagined that when Heavenly Father, Lord Jesus Christ and Holy Spirit see His children live in Godly harmony, how happy he would be. He would certainly pour out the blessings from heaven onto the government and churches to reward us, to encourage us!

I just want to see some day, the Lord Jesus Christ embrace us and say:

My children, well done, welcome home!

I think at that moment, I would be brought back to the years of Genesis, to hear our Heavenly Father's Word again after He created the heaven and earth and created us in His Almighty Image:

"And God saw that it was good."

(Genesis 1:10)

Be prepared to enter a new era of blessings

We are facing a severe economic crisis. On the one hand, we need to examine our previous weaknesses and failures, contain and prevent the existing economic system from further corruption. On the other hand, the U.S. needs to seek a new economic life, and run the race faithfully and joyfully in front of U.S.A.. We can not let the doom and gloom bury our dream and live in the past black hole and try to patch it under our old battle ground, we need a brand new way to boost our economic life both short term and long term.

Be prepared enter to a new era of blessings! Running for victory and becoming champions is my prayer for our nation.

First, we must be prepared in our spiritual realm. I believe, when we unify together under God, we will no fear any more; when we stand up again according to the Truth of God, we will have wisdom not only to solve the existing crisis, but also head to a new realm of Godly prosperities.

I believe, when we march on under the flag of Jesus Christ, the strength and wisdom will be granted to us, the signs and wonders will follow us. Americans and U.S. leaders will be more than conquerors.

> **"He who did not spare his own Son, but gave him up for us all-how will he not also, along with him, graciously give us all things?"**
>
> **(Romans:8:32)**

I believe there is nothing and no power will separate God and His children. There is nothing and no powers that will stop the help of God from reaching His earthly children. Once we lift our hands toward the heaven, he will answer our prayers. He will send us all we need, the wisdom and strength, to run the races of champions with us.

I believe, in this world, there are devils who are against God that have been thrown out from heaven to the earth by our Lord. They live with us in this world, and though our eyes may not see them, our spirit can feel their presence if we pay attention. But no matter however tricky and powerful the devil's strategy is, our God, the Jesus Christ is the Lord of lords, the King of kings, and His Almighty Power will help us overcome the power of the devils. His resurrecting power, which is stored in us, will be used to overcome any destroying plans from the evil ones.

> **"Who shall separate us from the love of Christ? Shall trouble or hardship or persecution or famine or nakedness or danger or sword?"**
>
> **(Roman: 8:35)**

"No, in all these things we are more than conquerors through him who loved us. For I am convinced that neither death nor life, neither angels nor demons, neither the present nor the future, nor any powers, neither height nor depth, nor anything else in all creation, will be able to separate us from the love of God that is in Christ Jesus our Lord."

(Roman: 8:37~39)

For the sake of all Americans, for the sake of the American dream, for the sake of fulfilling the government's responsibility to all Americans, which has ordained by God, I am going to share with you the treasures within our nation, which my soul can see the shining sparks and smell the sweet fragrant, the treasures will help Americans find the Hope in the dark tunnel and economic turmoil::

An America ARK

"He gives strength to the weary and increases the power of the weak. Even youths grow tired and weary, and young men stumble and fall; but those who hope in the Lord will renew their strength. they will soar on wings like eagles; they will run and not grow weary, they will walk and not be faint."

(Isaiah 40:29~31)

Theme II

It is the time to Build An American ARK

"Make yourself an ARK of gopherwood"

(Genesis 6:14)

"The kingdom of heaven is like a mustard seed, which a man took and planted in his field. Though it is the smallest of all your seeds, yet when it grows, it is the largest of garden plants and becomes a tree, so that the birds of the air come and perch in its branches"

(Matthew: 13:31~32)

An American ARK

can help the U.S. government solve the problem of unemployment
in a practical way and in an active approach

can help the Nation's Medical & Health Care dream come true

can build a broad transportation network in our nation
to reduce the usage of energy and create many benefits

can build, rebuild roads, bridges, school, state facility,
public facility, Americans' house etc. in a new way

can help the education system in many aspects

can reduce the Americans' living expense tremendously

can establish a new financial institutions system
by the people , for the people and for the benefit to the people

and more !

*Let me bring you to the realm of a new vision of strategy and method
for the US Economic Revival step by step*

---------------------------------- **Advocacy** ----------------------------------

Form A Non- Profit Industries And Services
Organization Group:
"An American ARK"

CONTRIBUTED BY THE PEOPLE,
FOR THE PEOPLE!

Besides U.S. Government administration system, I advocate U.S. Federal Government to form a Non-Profit Organization Group which is a comprehensive industries and services group, to enter into the Free Capital Market and Communities, to inject a strong boost of energy to the current economic system which is facing a great crisis.

This move of participation with a new vision , new strategy and method in the Free Capital Market and Communities will not only help our Government solve economic problems in the short term , but also help our nation's economic system to be an assuredly sustainable and healthy operation in the long term.

By An American ARK, the U.S. Government will fulfill the dream and responsibilities to take care of Americans not through debts but through creations. An American ARK will create nation's real assets and abilities to accomplish Government's multiple tasks, An American ARK will become nation's powerful vehicle driven by Faith, Hope and Love to serve the whole nation.

Structure and Function

<u>An American ARK</u> will supply sufficient job opportunities to entire nation, bring fresh and vital economic forces and sources to our nation, U.S. Federal Government financial system and State Government financial system if we can accomplish some of the following industry and service networks within our nation .

The scope of projects with market potential could be larger than what is listed below once we follow the needs in Free Capital Market and Communities.

Projects with market potential:

- An American ARK Medical & Health Care Network.
- An American ARK City Transportation Network.
- An American ARK Revival Construction Network.
- An American ARK Financial Institution Network.
- An American ARK Education Aids Network.
- An American ARK Preschool & Kindergarten Network.
- An American ARK Orphan Garden Network
- An American ARK Campus Health Food Supply Network.
- An American ARK Domestic Industries Revival Network. (includes: Light Industry, Heavy Industry)
- An American ARK House Investment & Development Network.
- An American ARK Elder Care & Living Garden Network and so on

The Sources of Fund:

Generally, the funds for the operation on each network could be the following sources, but it is not limited to:

- Government investment.

- Revenue from business operation in each network.
- Cross networks investment within An American ARK.
- Donation from American people as tax deductible contribution.
- Donation from American private enterprises as a tax deductible contribution.
- Profit re-investment.
  and so on

<u>An American ARK</u> is a business operation networks within Free Capital Market and Communities, but with the sole purpose which is for the sake of the people's and our nation's benefit, it is a love driven and responsibility driven organization of the U.S. Government.

I believe:

"On the mountain of the Lord it will be provided"

(Genesis 22:14)

Those who lives by "Faith, Hope, Love", who have generous and charitable heart, who care about our nation's future will be willing to support the U.S. Federal Government by action, to contribute their wealthy, works, efforts, talents etc with humility and honor, to build the "An American ARK" as a strong loving driven and responsibility driven forces to serve our country –U.S.A.

"In the same way, let your light shine before men,
that they may see your good deeds and
praise your Father in heaven"

(Matthew 5:16)

An American ARK vs. Free Capital Market and Existing System

<u>An American ARK</u> will let Americans have supports and opportunities to fulfill American dreams, live in peace, secure and endless hope, to experience God's goodness in our real life. Let the Government's tasks which can not be done through existing Free Capital Market be fulfilled.

<u>An American ARK</u> is a non-profit organization groups. It can be set up either on a fresh foundation or set up on a method called "horizontal foundation switch", which means, purchasing existing business from Free Capital Market by 100% ownership, base on its original structures, and set up a brand new systems.

<u>An American ARK</u> will enhance Free Capital Market's healthy operation, be a positive adjusting and balancing force to the undisciplined Free Capital Market, strengthen the positive function of Free Capital Market, help the weaknesses of Free Capital Market.

<u>An American ARK</u> will help U.S. Government reduce the cost, become more effective, more helpful, and provide more efficient services to Americans through active approach into the markets and communities.

<u>An American ARK</u> is the new era's strategy and method which can bring our nation's legacy and beauty together, model them to become a stable and solid vessel for Americans, help Americans live in a peaceful and blessed life, and be prepared to face and conquer crises.

<u>An American ARK</u> can establish a system to help those people who used to stay in the condition of "working poor" no longer poor, through different programs within An American ARK, let them get working reward to turn their unfortunate fate into a blessing.

An American ARK can establish a practical encouragement system to help those people who were used to or prefer live by Government's welfare to have working desire and opportunities to quit live in welfare, back to work and living in a life with real satisfaction, joy and hope.

An American ARK will establish " Second Chance" hiring and working system and environment to those who made mistake, who lived life in mess, who were cast away by the secular world------- let them have real second chance to rebuild their life in Godly path to fulfill American dream.

An American ARK will establish a system to promote "Honor Citizen" and "Working Ethic on Honor and Living", let people's good deeds be rewarded and be promoted.

An American ARK will set up reasonable compensations to all levels' employee, through different effective and efficient programs within whole networks to let employees reach the realm of living satisfaction.

An American ARK will establish a nationwide training system to training people's different skill for careers.

An American ARK can operate in a systematic, smooth, practical, healthy, fair, justice, and fresh way. It can help our Government undertake the un-shifting and ordained responsibilities to all American people.

An America ARK

will carry American people on a secured deck , sail on the midst of economic ocean side by side with Free Capital Market's ships or boats and private non-profit organization's ships or boats, help each other, learn from each other , encourage each other, cheer each other , run the race, cross the finishing line, fulfill the American dream.

Theme III

Explore An American ARK

"You will go out in joy and be led forth in peace"

(Isaiah: 55:12)

Part one: Explanations of five networks:

1. An American ARK Medical & Health Care Network:

will supply "Medical & Health Care" to whole nation without limitation, condition.

will supply "Medical & Health Care" to whole nation without burdens to people, firms and Governments;

will supply "Medical & Health Care" with quality, humility, effective, efficient, convenience functions;

It is a "Loving and Responsibility Driven Network" By People, For People!

(1) Blue Print and Vision:

- Establish " ARK City Clinic" to serve the community for minor & general sickness , the " ARK City Clinic" will include medical doctors, nurses, basic tests, mini pharmacy etc.

  "ARK City Clinic" is network's primary and essential component, it give patients initial and basic healing service and diagnoses, if there is a necessity , patient will be transferred

43

to "ARK County Hospital" for further comprehensive medical services. "ARK City Clinic" shall be set up according to demography. Small cities, may only have one "ARK City Clinic", in large cities, there may be more than one "ARK City Clinic".

"ARK City Clinic" can provide long hour services for the convenience to communities.

Due to high vacant rate in shopping center nationwide, every city can easily find proper location to build up "ARK City Clinic".

- Establish "ARK County Hospital" as the full professional medical service facilities by using existing public university's medical center which belong to or supported by State Government or Federal Government.

- Establish "ARK County Hospital" as the full professional medical service facilities by building new facilities or take over existing private hospitals.

- Establish "ARK County Hospital" as the full professional medical service facilities by sharing facilities or part of facilities with existing private hospitals. (only share facilities, not share management and service systems.)

- Focus on serious illnesses and treatment, "ARK County Hospital" may not accepted minor sickness, except emergency patient, "ARK County Hospital" may only accept the patient transferred from "ARK City Clinic" or from other medic professional for the serious sickness and treatment, such as operation and critical care.

- "An American ARK Medical & Health Care Network" should have own pharmacy located in "ARK City Clinic" and "ARK County Hospital" etc. to control and reduce the drug cost.

- Government needs to gradually walk out from the passive and negative position of paying "Insurance Premium" or pay charges of medical & health care to private provider. Build up the abilities to perform medical & health care tasks for Americans by strong functional medical & health care system ASAP. Turn the fact to pay unceasing soaring premiums or cost to private sector into making tangible, long term, non-risk investments in medical and health care sector.

- Government needs to discard the bondage of dependents on the private medical service providers which keeps making the medical industry cost dramatically climbing and out of control.

- Government needs an active approach to secure and undertake whole nation's medical & health care base on the strategy and method of " By Government Direct" through own tangible operation entities, simplify medical & health care management system to cut wasting cost, purchase drug directly, self control, self development, self management, own facilities, self employees etc. That means, there will be a medical & health care system which is totally separated with private system, serve the whole nation for the sake of people's medical needs.

- An American ARK Medical & Health Care Network will not only reduce financial burdens to government on Americans' medical cost, but also, create a healthy psychological environment (The lack of money and rise of cost will create anxiety and worries that can cause people to become more sick, being free from worry on medical cost may reduce the frequency of sickness. Worry and burden can cause people depression, etc.) Establishing an American ARK Medical & Health Care Network will strengthen people's health condition.

- An American ARK Medical & Health Care Network will set up a new professional medical and health care "Reasonable and Practical Standards" to avoid suffering and wasting service for patient, not only can reduce cost by omitting unnecessary medical procedures, but also to reduce patients painful experiences and respect patient's right and life.

- An American ARK Medical & Health Care Network will promote work ethic of " working for honor and living" within system, it will become a positive role model and example to leading people who have professional medical skills to serve the needs with good work ethic and willing to return the talent to community by honor.

- An American ARK Medical & Health Care Network will supply millions job opportunity to Americans besides private sector.

- An American ARK will design and operate whole networks with "Simplifying System Concept and Structure" to give Americans quality services. The simple structures will reduce cost tremendously and make service more effective and efficient.

(2) Financial Analyze:

Financial resources issue:

My suggestion is that An American ARK Medical & Health Care Network shall be designed as simple as possible. Let every one easily understand, join and enjoy the network for different kinds of benefits.

(All the data below are provided for the illustration purpose, they are all assumptions)

There are many financial resources to make this network work:

For example:

Contribution for American Adult, this part could support by:

- American own contribution
- Employer's contribution
- Government's Medicare and Medicaid fund
- If this part revenue for every American Adult is fixed $300/ month (every party can pay 1/3), the monthly revenue for American Adult will approximately be:

$45 billion per month

Contribution for American Children, this part could support by:

- Parents
- Parents' employer's contribution
- Government's Medicare and Medicaid fund
- If this part revenue for every American Child is fixed $100/ month (every party can pay 1/3), the monthly revenue for American Children will approximately be:

$15 billion per month

Total monthly fixed revenue= $60 billion

Adult contribution per visit(clinic or hospital):

Every adult pay: $40/ per visit
            $30/ for 30 days prescriptions.

Children per visit(clinic or hospital):

Every child cost: $30/ per visit.
            $20/ for 30 days prescriptions.

Poor family:

May pay nothing with city approved certificates or medic & health cost waiver card.

Other financial sources:

- Donations from individual charities or corporate donations etc. through fundraising programs as non-profit organization.
- Profit re-investment.
- Cross investment within An American ARK (please refer to An American ARK Financial Institution Network)
- Others.

Expenses issues:

- Build up clinic and hospital.
- Professional's compensation and other kinds of payrolls (non-professional positions).
- Drug purchasing cost.
- Facility, equipment expenses.
- Facility maintenance.
- Research investments for the university medical center or other medical research institutions.
- Others.

Example on revenue and expenses balance issue:

Next, I will give one example on revenue and expenses issues base on the term of contribution for American Adult and Children to see the potential of success in An American ARK medical and heath care system:

According the calculation above:

Total monthly fixed revenue= $60 billion

If, assuming every 100 Americans need 1 medical & health care professional, that's mean, the whole nation needs 3 million professional work for An American ARK Medical & Health Care Network (The professional include: medical doctor, nurse, assistant nurse, pharmacist etc.)

If, the average payroll for professional is $7000 per month:

The monthly payroll on professional=$ 21 billion

Difference: $ 60 billion-$ 21 billion=$39 billion will be used to cover other expenses.

What is the concept about $39 billion <u>per month</u>:

It can build **39000** "ARK City Clinic" (1 million cost),
or
It can build **390** "ARK County Hospital" (100 million cost)
or
It can build **39** "ARK County Hospital" (1 billion cost)

Wow! Think about that, if we add all the financial resources together, the fund will be:
- **Build up enough "ARK Clinic or Hospital"**
- **Hire millions professional and non professional.**
- **Let construction and related industries booming, millions additional job opportunities for Americans.**
- **Many other benefits!**

I believe, there are many ways can make this network works well as long as we work hard enough and dare to try.

(3) The Relationship:

What kinds relationship between An American ARK Medical & Health Care Network and Private Medical Service Suppliers, such as: Private Doctor Clinics, Hospital, and Insurance Company etc?

- "An American ARK Medical & Health Care Network" and Private Capital Medic Market shall exist in the market in parallel.

- "An American ARK Medical & Health Care Network" give all people the standard and quality medical treatments when they need it, supply the whole nation with real and necessary medical treatment without wasting, inconveniencing, or causing unnecessary suffering to the patients. When people need it, they will have it without burden, worry and hesitation.

- Private Medical Services is Free Capital Medic Market system which existing and operation under numerous reasons. There are many needs for this system exists. They will continuously play key roles in Medic Industry, side by side with "An American ARK Medical & Health Care Network" to serve the whole nation medical needs based on people's individual conditions.

- Since "An American ARK Medical & Health Care Network" is a Love and Responsibility driven medical system, it will let people get medical & health care under low cost, even no cost, also, will release all employers and governments' burdens on employee's medical & health care cost, this character also will effect Free Capital Medic Market system, positively influence them turn high cost and high profit realities to reasonable and market acceptable, let the people who used to and still want to get treatment from that system affordable.

- "An American ARK Medical & Health Care Network" is **Win-Win-Win program,** good for people either poor or rich, good for employers either business giants or small businesses, good for Government either Federal or States.

2. An American ARK City
Transportation Network:

can be designed as a
"square net's mass transportation system"
to provide people with convenience services and
many other benefits

(1) Blue Print:

- The transportation lines could be designed to cover and stop at every major streets and some minor streets inside city depending on demographics, such as residential areas, shopping area, school, library, senior citizen center, youth center, park, hospital , business center etc.

- The transportation lines need to be designed on high frequency stop.

- Set up " ARK City Control Center" and " ARK County Control Center" for parking , operation, controlling , directing, passages transfer, auto tools maintain etc.

- The transportation lines link "ARK City to City's Control Centers" with fast , very limited stop service to give the service to people who may need work in different city.

- The transportation lines link "ARK County to County's Control Centers" with fast, non-stop service to make long trips more faster.

The transportation lines link state to state bus station, train station, subway station, airport etc to create a big and diverse transportation net.

(2) Tools & Vision:

- Super duty van , such as FORD E 350 SUPER DUTY.

- This kinds vans which usually have 10 seats , can operated by basic class of drive license, that means that every driving person in America can easy qualify to be a "Van Driver" to serve the new and mass transportation network.

- Bus with different sizes:

Mini bus can be used within the city transportation net, like super duty van which I mentioned above. The regular size bus can be used on longer trips between "ARK City to City's Control Center", "ARK County to County's Control Center".

- Good effects on domestic auto industries and communities.

- In order to set up this network, government can **make orders from our domestic auto giants,** positively help them.

(3) Financial analyze:

My suggestion is that An American ARK City Transportation Network shall be designed as simple as possible. Let every one easily understand, join and enjoy the network for different kinds of benefits.

(All the data below are provided for the illustration purpose, they are all assumptions)

Win-Win-Win investments

If Government can give " Domestic Auto Giants" a order in the same amount as "Auto Bailout" fund: such as 30 billion dollars with bulk rate purchase on Van, we will get win-win-win result:

Assumption: U.S. Government invests 30 billion dollars to make an initial order to domestic auto giants instead of bail out plan, what will happen?

Government can get:

- Approximately 1,000,000 vans(1 million vans), such as FORD E-350 SUPER DUTY or similar size mini bus.

- 1,000,000 Vans for Network, that means:

1,200,000 people (1.2 million people) will have job (Drivers +Others) within 4000 cities, the calculation is as follows:

If a city with a population 50,000 needs 250 vans to fulfill a "square net", that means:

4,000 cities can establish "square net" on 30 billion dollars investment. 250 vans/per city x 4000 cities=1,000,000 vans

- Through different sources, when the funds are getting more and more, "square net" will become bigger and bigger, finally, whole nation will be covered. Meanwhile, we will save energy, reduce greenhouse gas and fight globe warming tremendously. This long term endeavor should be our task and responsibility.

- 1,000,000 Vans may let 100,000,000 people (100 million people) reduce the driving frequency, fuel demand will be reduced!

- Government can get revenue from operation (I will discuss this issue later)

Let's turn to another point, base on 30 billion dollars initial investments by U.S. Government to see what are the people and domestic industry's benefits:

Americans can get:

- 4000 cities will have convenience transportation network. People will enjoy life much easier.

- 1,000,000 Vans may release 100 million people from daily driving to occasional driving. Save fuel.

- 1.2 million New job opportunities.

- Many other benefits for families, such as save money and have more free time with family.

Auto giants can get :

- 30 billion is order rather than loan, three auto giants can perform production right away based on existing technology, employee, facilities etc. It may need minor modification on existing Van design in order to become public transportation tool, such as easy access for passengers, ticketing, van sign etc. For a period of technological innovation, the fuel efficient Van or Bus, environmentally friendly vehicles would be created.

- Auto Giants will keep employees.

- No headache on credit crash, no loan burden.

- Many other benefits, such as more abilities to appreciate and contribute to communities to fulfill capitalism's positive social dreams and more meaningful life.

Of course, the U.S. Government can take over auto giants who face crisis and willing to give up, with a total brand new operation and management system and 100% ownership, or the Government can build up a brand new Auto Factory by An American ARK, a non-profit organization.(please see the domestic heavy industry revival network)

Financial resources(Base on 4000 small cities)

Revenue from passengers' monthly pass:
- If $50 per person/ per month, Revenue will be :
  100,000,000 x $50= $ 5,000,000,000/ month
  That is: **$5 billion revenue per month**

Other financial sources:
- Donations from individual charities or corporate donations etc. through fundraising programs as non-profit organization.
- Profit re-investment.
- Cross investment within An American ARK(please refer to An American ARK Financial Institution Network)
- Others.

Expenses issues:

- Payroll expenses.
- Rent on facilities.
- Build facilities and maintain facilities.
- Build city van stops.
- Management and control center equipments etc.
- Van maintaining.
- Fuel.
- Others.

Example on revenue and expenses balance issue:

Next, I will give one example on revenue and expenses issues base on the term of Passengers' ticket sales to see the potential of success in An American ARK City Transportation Network:

According the calculation above:

Passengers' monthly pass revenue: $5 billion

If the average payroll is $3,000/per employee, the monthly payroll expenses will be:
1,200,000x$3000=3,600,000,000

Payroll for 1.2 million employee: $3.6 billion

Difference: $5 billion-$3.6 billion=$1.4 billion can be used to cover other expenses to make the network work well!

Anyway, by the An American ARK City Transportation network Government win, People win, Auto Industry win.

3. An American ARK City Revival
Construction Network:

will perform as a construction network to build, rebuild or remodeling roads, bridges, school, city or state facility, public facility, government's houses & apartments projects, and so on

(1) Blue Print:

- Set up a fresh system for evaluation, projecting, design, quotation, budgeting, purchasing, construction arrangement center for each of state or for Federal Government in public investment projects.

- Every County can have a Construction Branch, they undertake the projects within county or across the county for Government.

- Every State can have a Construction Coordinator Center to coordinate specific projects across the state or county. In this way, the sources could be used efficiently and coordinated effectively.

(2) Function and Purpose

- Reduce the cost through using this non-profit construction networks owned by the government rather than depending on private owned construction companies for government projects. We may rebuild more schools, we may remodel more bridges, roads and streets, we may remodel more of the government's facilities to save energy, we may build more parks for the people, we may build decent houses and apartments with low costs for Americans, we may build nice and professional care & living communities for the elders with low costs. Anyways, An American ARK Revival Construction Network will let more city and more people to be benefited from the U.S. Government's large public investment.

- Supply stable and secured job opportunities, advocate working ethic for honor and living.

- Centralize purchasing or stocking can make material cost lower.

- Long term maintain on the public facilities consistently and systematically.

- Quality control and timing control more directly and easily.

- Make certain Government's investment or taxpayer's money more effectively, more efficiently and more productively.

— 4. An American ARK Education Aids Network —

will help children get more education,
talent guidance and support;
help children live in safe & secure environment;
help working parents to take care children;
provide more job opportunity to university student through this after
school aids network.

(1) Ideas:

- In public school ,set up extension classes and activity club for every student if they want to stay or have to stay for their personal reasons after regular school time. such as from 3:00 pm to 7:00 pm in every school day.

- Help children to arrange their spare time more meaningfully rather than spend several hours in computer or game when they stay home alone.

- Reducing working parents' worrisome on children in this modern time.

- Establish this education aids system more effectively and functionally to help children stay in school after regular school hours to learn and enjoy positive social activities rather than stay in a simple day care after school.

- The extended classes or diverse clubs will help children to learn more in their interesting or talent fields, such as : reading, writing , math, speech, music, sports, performing arts, drawing, cooking, computer, science, politics, community services, academic competition, talents competition, etc. these classes or clubs will be run by An American ARK Education Aids Network under school attentions and in cooperation with school.

- The Network can hire university students, not only let university students have chance to earn college tuition, but also let them positively help and encourage young children to learn more about the future education opportunities and admission examination, such as SAT.

- The Network also can provide more job opportunities to qualified talents, teachers, even parents with high education background, through certain qualification system to get more qualified people to help our young generation to grow healthy, to help their life more colorful and active. Advocate the work ethic within network is for honor and for living.

- Within school district, set up extreme talented student center to support those kinds children in whole district, let their talent be better developed.

- Set up more school bus lines to pick up and delivery students for the parent's convenience. An American ARK city transportation system may fulfill the needs.

- Family can contribute $200/month for a child to let their child learn more, stay in a safety and at the convenience of a parents' working schedule. For low income family, this charge could be waived.

(2) Goal:

- Help our young generation find their nature talent & life potential , build up their confidence in the future careers.

- Help our young generation realize their social responsibility, to family , to community, to nation.

- Help our young generation more discipline in life and learn the art of life management before they grow up.

- Stir up our young generation's inner gifts and encourage them dare to dream for a meaningful life.

- Preparation aids to children for advance education opportunities. Reduce parents' burdens.

- Help the relationship enhancement between children and their parents. Support children as well as parents.

5. An American ARK
Financial Institution Network:

is a total fresh financial institution system under
Government total control and operation
besides private financial institution,
under health regulation and health market strategy ,
under the purpose of protection and management
for American's wealth and life source

(1) Ideas:

- Establishing total fresh financial institution on commercial banking sector and on investment banking sector. Making active approach into Free Capital Financial Market.

- Set up simple service structure, system and products, make system more transparent, effective and more productive to Government and to Americans.

- Establishing "An American ARK Bank" over nationwide to serve the consumers.

- Operation under a healthy regulation system which can avoid and prevent the previous mistakes in Free Capital Finance Market happen again.

- Manage and invest people's money or government's money in conservative and safe way by investing the projects within An American ARK, such as, the public projects, domestic industries projects, medical and health care network, transportation network, education network, house and apartment project etc. those projects undertaken by government.

- Establish a financial service circle with simple and non-risk pattern, such as: consumer basic banking service, invest consumer's saving on government's projects for Americans, reward reasonable interest to consumers. Make the financial system running as simple as 1-2-3, avoid complicated business products and activities.

- Let Americans' money create good projects through U.S. Government's hands; Let Americans' money working for Americans; Keep Americans' money in safety and invest it productively; Let Americans purchase moderate houses, condos and apartments with affordable and no-burden price. Let Americans' live in peace and security.

- Fill the absent or empty spots in financial market due to private bank's bankruptcy or out of business, let people have new job opportunities, let the consumers have new and trustable banks to give them further services.

(2) Goal:

- U.S. Government take action, plant a good seed to ground, use more   active strategy and method to solve and prevent economic crisis in short term and in long term.

- Enter to the Free Capital Finance Market , play a key role, be a good model , to leading, to guiding, to operate, to regulate , to positively influence the most important market of a nation's life-financial sector. Side by side , hand in hand with the private finance capital, to run a healthy finance race. Let the "American Finance Team" win the race in " The World Finance Olympics"

- Sowing a tremendous powerful good economic seed in our fertile and vast land, we will have a wonderful harvest!

Part two: Introduction of seven networks:

The following fields are directly related to people's basic and essential life. They are: Food, House, Transportation, Energy, Education, Medical, Finance etc. Some of them I already discussed before. Now, I am going to discuss more networks within **An American ARK** which are worthy for the government to invest and get revival.

— 1. An American ARK Light Industries Network: —

- Reviving various light industries districts which are worthy to be re-boosted, be developed base on region's industry history, set up brand new domestic industries or purchase existing domestic industries etc. with 100% ownership.

- Through the revival on domestic light industries, create more job opportunities.

For example:

An American ARK Food Manufactory & Distribution Network:

- Develop and manufacture healthy food for family, school, hospital, church, charity, etc.

- Establish the food industry circles and districts from farms to finishing products.

There are many domestic light industries are worthy to revive according to consumers' needs. Think and Try!

— 2. An American ARK Heavy Industries Network: —

The heavy industries are the key strengths for a nation's economy. Oil & Energy, Auto, Airplane and other transportation tools, etc all belong to heavy industries and are worthy for the U.S. Government to invest and take revival action in.

For example:

An American ARK Oil & Energy Industry Network

- Government undertake this most important industry for a nation and people in heavy industries sector is very important to a nation's benefits either on short term or long term.

- Oil & Energy Manufactory is a massive investment and high tech industries, a healthy Oil & Energy industry system needs strong diverse sources and elements to get together, depending on private capital to make this industry work well, is not enough due to the capitalism's limitation. Government has more sources and strength to develop this industry well, compared with private capital.

- It is better that the U.S. Government enter into this most important industry ASAP, to play a key role, from research to manufacture, from regulation to control, be prepared to have a strong active ability to solve nation's crisis on Oil and Energy sector, to have the "Sense of Urgency" and " Sense of Crisis", to develop more efficient and effective ways to meet the nation's energy needs.

- Create long term and secured job opportunities to Americans.

- Government not only become independent on this industry, also help Free Capital Market to balance, adjust, and leading whole heavy industries into a health path.

3. An American ARK House Investment & Development Network:

Seeing the house crisis having taken place in the U.S.A. and the ridiculous climbing rents on apartments, I think the house market is a very important market where U.S. Government should consider entering into, to reduce the people's living cost, to help Americans not only to have a decent place to live, but also live in a healthy way without financial bondage.

An American ARK House Investment & Development Network

Will let Americans have homes to live in

- U.S. Government enters into house market to build up affordable and decent house or apartments either sale to the people or lease to the people.

- Government intervenes this market and play key role under the non-profit motivation for the people's sake. Through the "An American ARK City Revival Construction Network", the Government can build houses or apartments with low cost compared with Private builders.

- Government can develop certain financial support plans to help people buy house through new financial aids: "Non-Debt Method" and " Debit Release Method", to help the people in a creative way and a bondage-free choice to buy home.

- This network could be developed together with other An American ARK networks, not only give people various and diverse job opportunities, but also, let them have decent and affordable homes to live in.

- Intervening in house market and building affordable house and apartment for the people, government's active approach will influence whole market back to healthy and reasonable condition according to the Free Market automatic adjustment principle.

- Government will create tremendous job opportunities in construction sectors, real estate sector and related industries.

I believe, this is a win-win project, good to people, good to Government.

4. An American ARK Elder Care & Living Garden Network:

I had some chances to observe the systems about senior citizens' living and elders' assistant living. Same as depending on private medical & health care suppliers, there are many disadvantages within the elderly people's living sector. The worrisome reality is that it is very costly for U.S. Government and families.

I advocate:

U.S. Government to build and to manage elder care & living facilities directly. It may reduce the cost to American, Federal Government, State Government by 30% to 50% through establishing government owned non-profit organization:

An American ARK Elder Care & Living Garden Network

- Government works out to build senior citizen living garden and elder assistant living garden, letting our parents or grandparents spend the rest of their life with quality living care, quality medical and health care, letting our parents or grandparents live in a loving environment without heavy financial burden.

- Through loving and professional services, to appreciate our parents' and grandparents' efforts and love for descending generations and our country, to help them still enjoy their life and fulfill the American dream.

- Base on "To Build and Manage by Government" concept, the cost will be reduced. Government can create more job opportunities and give our parents and grandparents better quality services.

Some day, when our parents or grandparents leave this world, they will carry the peace with them, they will carry the dignity with them, they will carry all the loving memories with them.

This is my faith ,hope and prays for our parents and grandparents.

5. An American ARK Preschool & Kindergarten Network

The very beginning education and care are the most important elements and investments in human being's life.

Due to the present condition, in most families, both parents need to work , the child either be sent to a home care which may not be a very safe environment , enough educated backgrounds, enough helping hands, etc. or be sent to a private preschool and kindergarten which may cost parents $700 or more per month.

I advocate:

An American ARK preschool and kindergarten network

to give our children more professional care and love,
to give parents supports and reduce financial burden,
to create more job opportunities.

Ideas:

- Base on every city, establish public profession preschool and kindergarten with low cost to family, such as $300 per child each month and free for poor family, help family save more than 50% cost on each child comparing with private preschool and kindergarten.

- Let child get stander, professional education and care at their beginning age of life.

- Let working parents not only enjoy their child, but enjoy their work, let families' child care and education cost be reduced, let low income families have abilities to let children get quality and standard education opportunity.

- Create city based job opportunities.

6. An American ARK
Orphan Garden Network:

I hope all orphans can have a beautiful, sweet, warm, safe home with a abundant love.

Children are like little trees or flowers, the ground we plant them in is absolutely important, the ground will effect their whole life, especially to orphans, they don't have a mother and father. The U.S. Government should become their legal parents to take care of them with more care and love.

I advocate:

Besides the existing foster families system and private charity orphanages, U.S. Government to build:

An American ARK Orphan Garden Network

For our orphans and abandoned children with good environment and standard professional management.

- Government gathers the sources together, let orphans or abandoned children at least have another fair choice besides existing systems to live in a loving and standard care environment like a normal child or even with better care and better education, let them have a chance to become gifted and talented children with uplifted spirits.

- Once the child living in Garden, people with loving heart still can be their foster parents, like a normal family sending child to a boarding school, at weekend, they can be pick up to their foster parents home to enjoy normal family loving life.

- Let the children with poor beginning, ending in blessing, let our nation and government get blessing through their blessing, take U.S. government's responsibility in a active way.

- Create job opportunities to those who love to take care of children, who have professional teaching talents, who have children care skills.

- Put sincere efforts to raise those unfortunate children, help them pursue a higher education and be prepared for a future career. They don't have parents, so the Government and those who have a loving heart may become their parents to take care of them in their spiritual life and physical life.

They are the Apples in God's eyes, I pray for orphans and abandoned children that they may have a sweet home in which to live and grow.

7. An American ARK Campus
Healthy Food Supply Network:

For decades, the life environment has been affected by consumer products. The unhealthy food not only occupies grocery stores, family tables, fast food stores, but also occupies our schools' lunch tables--- unhealthy food has become part of our life style. The unhealthy food poisons our physical body, also gradually and quietly changing our family values and unity.

School is the place to educate our children, life style is an important practical lesson in the school system, "Food" they eat in school will gradually cause them to become " Used to" and "Addicted to" unhealthy foods. We need do something for our children.

I advocate:

An American ARK School Healthy Food Supply Network

- Engage in developing and manufacturing healthy foods for our school system, let our children eat healthy, drink healthy and study healthily.

- This Network can work together with the Network which I mentioned in light industries: "An American ARK Food Manufacture and Distribution Network", to help and serve schools, families and communities.

**Yes, I see there are tremendous markets and ways
to help Americans and U.S.A. Government
to fulfill
the American Dream and overcome the economic
crisis through the Non-Profit organization :
An American ARK**

An American ARK

will be new wine, its sweet fragrance
will fly and become
positive and strong elements in our nation's economic system.

"No one sews a patch of unshrunk cloth on and old garment,
for the patch will pull away from the garment, making
the tear worse. Neither do men pour new wine into old
wineskins. If they do, the skins will burst, the wine will
run out and the wineskins will be ruined, No, they pour
new wine into new wineskins, and both are preserved"

(Matthew:9:16~17)

My Soul Can See

My soul can see:
In USA capitol, congress hall,
All USA leaders, they stand together,
their hands touch their heart, the tears in their eyes,
the vows come from their heart,
like a series symbols flying to sky,
the sparking symbols get together,
so strong , so strong, like a strong wind,
flying in to a silver , shining sparking receiver.

My soul can see:
the receiver with a label
---- Earthly No 1 Receiver---
---Property of Heaven---
Oh, once the hearts start to speak,
the sounds become sparking symbols to fly,
the receiver starts to record,
every word, every mind
which comes from the leaders' heart who are vowing:

"We the people of the United States,
in order to form a more
perfect union,
establish justice,
insure domestic tranquility,
provide for the common defense,
promote the general welfare,
and secure the blessings of liberty,
to ourselves and our posterity,
do ordain and establish this constitution for the

United States of America"
"I pledge allegiance to the flag
of the United States of America,
to republic, for which it stands,
one nation, under God, invisible,
for liberty and justice for all"

my soul can hear:
there is a sound like a wing surrounding

their vowing continuously,
the sparking symbols flying,
the receiver is recording :

"We are the U.S. leaders, the servants of U.S. citizen,
Once a while, we separated by parties,
Now, we become one, one united party
under God.
We know, we are ordained by God ,
not to be served, but to be a honor servant to
God's people.

We know, we are elected by people,
under God's free will Law,
have the responsibility to people, and to God

We know, we are created by God,
we are different,
different race, different gender, different color,
different background, different talent, different ability,
different responsibility.

God is the creator, He created me in His image, not a robot,
so,
we are different by His artistic craftsman hands
He looks at our teamwork, He will say
' It is good' as what He said when I just be created
' It is good', ' It is good', ' It is good'

yes, ' It is good'
we do differently
but, we are whole, when we stand together, work together
under God

We know, we are ordained by God, elected by people,
now, we are standing here, a holy and honored place,
not to do for our own sake,
but for people's sake, for God's sake
we will be granted by a honored crown by people
we will be embraced by God's greeting:
Well done, my faithful servant!
yes, He said:
'If you did on the least, you are done for me.'

we start to realize this is the true comfort ,
reward and satisfaction
more than anything else in the world
indeed.

We know we are brothers and sisters standing here,
a holy and honored place
a headquarter of the blessing operation
we need to respect each other,
we need cheer up each other,
we need to pray for any one's weakness,
we need to support anyone's weakness to make this
leadership body whole.

We know, from generation to generation,
from pilgrims to 300 million people,
from president to president
from congress to congress
we are like a team in the athletic race,
to run the race for the nation,
to lead the race for our people.

we are gradually learned ,
in our team, there are someone may be slow,
there are someone may fall,
but, we need to see them as God see them,
nothing can make the team strong,
only
love and encouragement to each other can
make our leadership team whole,
make the nation and people strong,
make our forefather and our dream come true.

we are gradually learned,
nobody is perfect, nobody is a superman,
but, when we love each other, learn each other,
help each other, joined each other,
we may get to be more perfect,
we may run closer and closer to our destiny,
we may finish a superman task,
we may run the race by victory.

we are gradually learned,
we are brothers and sisters in Lord,
when anyone falls or gets sick
it is just like myself falling and getting sick,
blaming each other, the team will fall apart,
in the athletic race field,
the stick in our hands may fall,
the next hands may shake,
the race can not be finished.

we know, God is in control,
if we see the people , see the leader
by God's eye, by God's feeling
we will see, every generation, every president ,
every leaders, every one
has certain legacy left
for the purpose of good
for God's people
and for God's glory.

we are gradually learned,
once the nation is going to face uncertainness,
but, God knows,
He is always in control for the nation who trusts Him,
He ordained our leaders in the particular time,
to have the strength and wisdom to face the future.
remember, He never loses control.

we are gradually learned,
since we are one body under God.
one part pain, our whole body suffering,
why not , to be a angel to heal the painful part,
let the whole body healthy
in God's eye.

we believe, if we do so,
His satisfaction on our team ,
will pour out His blessing from heaven to
our nation , our leader, our people,
we will see His smile over the sky,
we will hear the heavenly rejoice melody,
we will see His stretching hands from heaven down to earth to
embrace our nation like before.

We know, His blessing only pours upon :
the poor in spirit,
those who mourn,
the meek,
the one who hunger and thirst for righteousness,
those who are merciful,
those pure in heart
those who are peacemaker,

those who are persecuted because of righteousness.

so, let us hand in hand, side by side,
to encourage each other,
to unite together,
send our team prayer to Almighty God
to be ready to receive His truly blessings.

we gradually learned,
we can not forget our nation's root,
our foundation,
our dream,
our purpose,
our destiny,
if we forget, or abandon it,
just like:
we lost our true identity which is who we are,
just like:
we lost our strength,
we lost our blessing,
we lost our true nature meaning,
we may lost all

through our trial,
through nation's hundreds years history,
through our pain,
we gradually learned
we are losing the most precious dream
through the deny in truth;
we are losing our best to exchange back
with the vain , vain , vain,
empty, empty, empty.
the darkness is blinding our eye,
destroying our taste, confusing our value,
forgot who we are,
where we came from,
what should we do here,
where we are heading to----

Oh, God,
this is not right, this is not right,
we even don't know
from where, from when, from which generation,
we had been lost.
look at the mess, look at the scars,
this is not what we want, this is not what we dreamed,
please show the path to us as you see.
we really want our dream back,
we really want our heart be truly in rest

Oh, God
we think we are strong, but we are getting weak,
we think we are rich, but we are getting poor,
because we are losing our abundant source,
that is You, our God
who brought us to this land with dream and faith.

Oh, God
we still remember you told us the old stories,
a prodigal son back to Father's home,
the blind man , be healed
the leprosy woman , be healed and cleaned,
yes,
there are thousands and thousands old stories reminded us
You are yesterday, today, and tomorrow, never change.

Oh, God
we remember, you said:
'come to me, all you who are weary and burdened,
and I will give you rest,
Take my yoke upon you and learn from me,
for I am gentle and humble in heart,
and you will find rest for your soul,
for my yoke is easy and my burden is light.'

Yes, God
we are tired, your people are tired,
we can not wander and fall to destruction any more
please release our burden, and your people's burden,
they are my brothers, they are my sisters.

if they pain, I am really feeling pain,
if they cry, I am really feeling to cry with them,
oh, I know, my heart tell me,
we are brothers and we are sisters,
we are the one body under God.

Oh, God
You gather us together in this land with your purpose
because we have same destiny.
as a nation's leaders,
we can not just take care ourselves well,
and leave my brothers and sisters, your people in sorrow,

If I am doing so, thinking so, I have no rest,
Someday, I can not go to see you, my Father,

I will feel shame, real shame,
I will feel sorry, real sorry,

I can not answer your question:
'where is your other brothers and sisters?'
I can not just tell you:
oh, Father, they are sound poor and sick,
I left them in earth.

Oh, God
although we are mess up with many, many things,
we know one key Hope message ,
it is not too late to come to you now,
we don't know
if it is too late to come back to you by tomorrow,
because we don't own the time,
but, at least I know, today is not too late
to ask for forgiveness,
the light, the truth, and the way.

Oh, God
once we stand here, bring our memories
from yesterday to today,
who can deny the dream which
makes me, leads me, strengthens me,
encourages me to stand here is not
planed by you, my God?
who can boastly stand here to say
this is not the God's favor for the purpose of people's sake?

Oh, God
we can not forget our dream and the dream maker,
we can not just look for the blessing
and forgot the one who gives us blessing,
that's you, my Father, my God!
we can not just say we are the nation
under God but actually forgot our God,
even can not describe what He looks like .

Oh, God
we don't want to put you in our closet anymore ,
we can not stand to putting you in our closet anymore
we can not hide you in our secret place,
we cry out to you to hide us under your
almighty wings , your secret place,

If we lock you in our closet,
feel shame to preach your name,
we lock the nation's strength,
we lock the nation's wisdom,
we lock the nation's dream,
we lock the nation's blessing.
we lock the nation's truth,
only your truth can set us free.

Oh, God
we are totally up side down,
why our nation is hiding our true strength,
show the world our substituted strength,
who we want to satisfy?
who we want to please?
how foolish we are, how foolish we are!

Oh, God
did we ignore your reminder and wake up call?
did you treat our foolish attitude by your humor?
if not,
why we sleep so deep , so long?

Oh, God
we know, you are humor,
you are full of Love
but , also we know you have the nature of wrath,
just like you said:
'As many as I love I rebuke and chasten.'

Oh, God
If we have ever rebellion in your eye,
we want to say sorry, a very deep sorry to you.
please forgive us , please give us second chance,
please give us the truth.

Oh, God
you may say
you have given us so many and so many chances
but, we ignore or pretend never heard,
please give us one more chance,
please save us from perish.
our forefather vowed, we vowed,
we are the nation under God,
we will not deny what we vowed,
we will not show You and the world
double faces.

Oh, God
we don't want the strength
you give to Samson left us just like left him,
since he cut his ordained hair from you
by devil's deceiving,
we will keep the hair You ordained,
we will keep the dream you planed,
please, do not withdraw the strength
you give to Samson from us, please.

Oh, God
not only that,
we want the strength you give to Gideon, give to us,
through that strength,
he conquered thousands and thousand enemy by 300 solders,
our nation is facing thousands and thousands difficulties now,
every difficulties seems like a enemy which Gideon faced.

Oh, God
we try to interpreted and apply the old story
to our modern time,
we try use science to analyze your almighty work,
but, we realize,
if the human mind can interpret how you did for Gideon
if the science can figure out what you did on Gideon's case
how can we give the definition of Miracle?
how can we give the definition of Almighty?

The more we try to figure out, the more we get confused
because you said:
'without Faith, never please God'

Oh, God
we walk to you now by Faith, by Hope , by Love
even though you are invisible,
but, we believe, with you
nothing is impossible
we remember you teaching us about the
Faith of a mustard seed,
with that Faith,
Mountain can be moved, Storm can be stopped,
of course, our nation's crisis
will be conquered

Oh, God
You must have heard,
not only the nation's leaders pray to you,
we have beautiful people who never give up to trust you ,
they are praying now
to seek the highest counselor , you, our God.

we can not forget the people who send us to this position
by their trust and loving heart and expectation,
we can not play our role like playing game,
we have great responsibility to stand here,
we have great dream to fulfill
rather than
the power , fame and money which the world seeks,

We are the God's servant, God's ambassador,
what great honor.

We know, through our work,
people will enjoy your original design life for them,
live here like living in heaven.

we know, if only:
I am not in hunger, I am not unclothed,
I am not unsecured,
I am not homeless, I am not lone, I am not lack,
I am not sick, I am not jobless,
I am not in debt,
I am not single mother, I am not single father,
I am not lone elder,
I am not uneducated, I am not helpless,
Then:
I am a successful almighty leader of U.S.A.
will become
a lie message,
a false feeling,
a deceiving power,
a destruction,
a departing path from my original design to
be a servant for God and people,
a departing path from my blessing.

Because, we know,
if I earned the whole world, but lose our soul
we lose all"

My soul can see:
the party wears red gown , the gown is falling,
the white gown appear with shining and sparking;
the party wears blue gown, the gown is falling,
the white gown appear with shining and sparking;
the party wears green gown, the gown is falling,
the white gown appear with shining and sparking;
all kinds colorful gown , is falling , is falling,
the white gown appear with shining and sparking
cover the all U.S. congress hall.

My soul can see:
the real joy comes to their face,
the real peace comes to their face
the real dream comes to their face,
the real child smiles, the real child smiles with tears
come to their face.
the chain, the shackles of
the hate, the jealous,
the regret, the sorrow, the unjust, un-forgiveness ,
the fear, the hiding, the self centered, the self ambition,
the self gain, the dark power , the dark controlling,
the dark manipulating, the dark competition,
the dark idolatry,
the dark judgmental, ----- oh,
all kinds dark chains, shackles are falling and falling ,
disappeared and disappeared from the surface .

My soul can see:
The leaders, they look at each other with a peaceful smile,
they look at each other with tear and joy.

my soul can see:
they are talking to each other :
"we love the U.S.A. nation, the people, and God
we realize the beautiful dream draws every one here for purpose,

we realize what's the wonderful combination team
if the team is no pride , no prejudice

we realized,
if we fight each other within the team
to protect one's life rather than
sacrifice living for other, we may lose our life,
because
we been called as a servant for each other.
we been called as a giver to the people,
not be greedy receiver.
the royal blood floating in our vain, finalize, finalize,
from inside to our surface,
we hiding the most precious treasury,
we ignore our most marvelous earthly task,
Oh, we were blind,
now, we can see;
we forgot,
now, we remember
our divining, pointed, ordained life meaning as a leader,
political law maker and servant
for U.S.A. nation and for the world"

my soul can see:
there are hundreds of beautiful, white doves.
standing on our nation leader's shoulders.
leaders are exciting, they are talking to each other:
"look, my brother, there is a dove in your shoulder---
Oh, my brother, my eye can see
there is a dove in your shoulder too"
yes, they find out, the one standing with a new white gown,
all standing there with a dove,
a wisdom counselor and comforter sending
by God.
He answers our leader's prayer
He descends the blessing to our nation.

my soul can see:
our nation's leaders with new white gown,
they be cheering up,
they tearing, they smiling, they hugging ,they praying
they lift their humble hands towards heaven ,
give thanks to God

my soul can see:
they became the one of most beautiful child,
their original dream be stirred up,
their faith be lift up,
they have the real confidence to leading our nation
to run the race,
to cross the final line
to win the life champion .

oh, my soul can see,
my soul can hear,

my heart just wants to sing and dance with the joy
for the wonderful U.S.A. leadership union celebrating.

~ End~

"For God so loved the world that
he gave his one and only Son,
that whoever believes in him
shall not perish but have eternal life"

(John: 3:16)